T0131788

Justin's Jesus

MARY SWICK

WESTBOW
PRESS
A DIVISION OF THOMAS NELSON

WestBow Press books may be ordered through
booksellers or by contacting:

WestBow Press
A Division of Thomas Nelson
1663 Liberty Drive
Bloomington, IN 47403
www.westbowpress.com
1-(866) 928-1240

ISBN: 978-1-4497-3616-3 (sc)
ISBN: 978-1-4497-3615-6 (e)

Library of Congress Control Number: 2011963688

Printed in the United States of America

WestBow Press rev. date: 01/06/2012

At that time Jesus, full of joy through the Holy Spirit, said, "I praise you, Father, Lord of heaven and earth, because you have hidden these things from the wise and learned, and revealed them to little children. Yes, Father, for this was your good pleasure."

-Luke 10:21

Contents

Dedication

I would like to dedicate this book to the Lord, Jesus Christ, for carrying us through this storm and showing us He is big enough to handle our pain and conquer our biggest fears.

In loving memory of Justin, I miss you everyday precious baby, but I know that Jesus is holding you in his arms. I can't wait until we are able to see you again and hold you in our own arms.

To my wonderful husband, Ryan, who has been there with me through thick and thin; you have been my rock, my shoulder to cry on, and even on my worst days, the sweetest man I know.

To Riley and Jacob, you boys mean so much to me, and I am so proud to be your mommy.

To every parent, grandparent, and sibling who has had a child go to Heaven long before you desired; and in loving memory of those children.

To Justin Kniefl, Ben Holbrook, Tyler Bird, Jarid Anderson, Keeley Settles, Dakota Cleland, and Dacey De Whitmire, may you all be dancing among the angels and watching over your families.

Acknowledgements

I would like to extend a huge thank you to everyone who has been there for us through this trying time. I cannot believe the amount of support we received from so many people and communities. To the EMT's, First Responders, Eric and Jessi Eugenio, for all your help that day!

To everyone who brought covered dishes and supplies after Justin's funeral, we thank you from the bottom of our hearts.

Thank you to Pastor T.J Norman, his wife Laurie, and all of the people of the First Christian Church in Iowa Falls.

To Leonard Linn, and the Linn Funeral Home staff, you all have been such a godsend to us. Thank you so much for all you have done

To both Ryan's parents and mine, thank you so much for instilling in us a strong faith, for taking us to church, and providing us with a solid foundation in Jesus Christ.

Thank you to my dad for making me get out of bed all those Sunday mornings to go to church; even though I wasn't happy about it then, I appreciate it more than you know!

To all of our sisters, you have been so amazing to both of us. The Strength, dedication, and love you have shared are truly a treasure to us both.

Many, many, thanks to my sister Jill Brindle, and Jack Dennis, who always seemed to find time to spend with us and with the boys especially during the crucial times in our lives. Thank you so much for staying with me while Justin was in the NICU, for staying to help with swimming lessons, and for staying with me after Justin's funeral. You have been there for us through everything and I cannot express my appreciation and love enough. Thank you so much! We love you!

Thank you to those of you who helped in getting *Justin's Jesus* ready for publishing. Joni Irlmeier, you are such an amazing lady, I was so blessed to have you as a teacher and I cannot begin to express my gratitude and appreciation. Thank you for being willing to do the editing for us on *Justin's Jesus*. Thank you also for introducing the name "Ryker" to me, I love that name!

Thank you to my cousin Leigh Rigby-Adcock for doing the final editing. I cannot begin to express my appreciation and gratitude!

To my Great-Aunt Marilyn who also edited *Justin's Jesus*, thank you so much for your time, we love you.

Thank you to my grandmother, Martha Havens, for all you did and brought for us after Justin's passing, and thank you so much for giving us the privilege of keeping

Justin so close to us, by letting us use the burial plots; we are eternally grateful. Love you.

To my Aunt Janie, who came as soon as she heard the news and stayed with us. Thank you for helping us laugh during such a hard time, easing the tension, and calming us down I am so grateful for your constant support. You have always been there for me, and I cannot thank you enough!

To my Aunt Gina for being there for us while hearing the awful news. Thank you so much for your love and support, I could not have done it without you!!!

To my grandparents, who mean the world to me: thank you for all you have done for us, and all the lessons you have taught us; you are an inspiration and great living example of love, generosity, and kindness. We love you!

Thank you to Stephanie Stolzman for all you did for us after Justin's passing and the support you have given us. You are a great person, a wonderful friend, and an amazing boss.

To my best friend, Amanda Holbrook, and her mother Cheryl, who has always been like a mother to me. You two ladies have been such a big part of my life; thank you so much for everything. I love you both!

To Bruce and Rhonda Kniefl, thank you for sharing with us not only your son's name and legacy, but your story and your hearts as well.

Deb and Larry Anderson, thank you so much for meeting with us the day after Justin went to be with Jesus, I will cherish that night forever! You are such an inspiration to the both of us. I am so glad that Justin gets to be so close to your son, both in Alden and in Heaven, I'm sure.

We probably forgot to mention a number of people, please know that we are so thankful for every single one of you whom God has placed in our lives; we cherish each of you.

Letters to Justin

JUSTIN,

There are so many things I want to say to you. I never thought I would have to write them in a book, I just always thought I would be able to tell you. As much as I worried that this would happen, once it did, I was at a loss as to what to do next. You are, and always have been, so precious to me. I think about you every day as if you were here. I wonder what I would put you in to wear that day; if your hair would always be so baby soft or if you would lose it; and if I could cover you in baby lotion forever, just so you would smell the way you did when we first brought you home.

I snuggle with your blanket, I rub it across my face, the same way you liked to fall asleep; it still smells like you. I miss you so much that I can't even begin to put it into words. I know you are happy in Heaven, and you are in the care of so many amazing people, but I've got to say, sometimes I still wish you were in my care. My arms feel empty without you in them. I see a baby in church, or at the store, and my heart breaks for me, and yet I am so happy for their mommies and daddies who are still able to hold their babies in their arms.

I hate so many things about you being away from us. I hate that my arms are empty. I hate this hole in my heart. I hate not being able to watch you grow up, feel your hugs, your kisses, or hearing you say the words, "I love you, Mommy".

There are so many things I want to see you do, hear you say, and be proud of you for, but I want you to know that, little one, I am so proud of you! I am so proud to be your mommy, and there are so many things I am happy about also! I am so glad I got the chance to feel you in my arms, to hear you giggle in your sleep, to see your smile, to smell your hair, touch your skin, and watch you roll over. I don't remember the sound of your cry, and that's okay because you don't cry in Heaven. I am so thankful to have a baby in Heaven, I am so glad you will not feel any pain, that you live among rainbows and light, that you are always happy, and what better place to live than among Jesus and his angels.

I miss you, Justin, and I always will, but I have peace in my heart knowing that Jesus is keeping you safe in his arms until I can see you again. Please watch over your brothers, sometimes they get into more mischief than even I can handle. I love you so much. I still buy things for you, we talk about you every day, and you are in all of our prayers every night. Please ask Jesus to let you keep your soft baby hair so that I can rub my face against it when I get the chance to see you again. And please know that if it is in God's plan that we are ever blessed with another child, that the special place we have for you in our hearts will never filled by any other. You are amazing and wonderful to u; you always have been and always will be. Please give that new baby kisses before sending him or her to us. I find comfort in knowing that you will be with your brother or sister before we ever get to hold them in our arms. There are so many people, who love and adore you, and I cannot even imagine how many lives you have touched, you really have been a work of God and again, I am so proud of you! I love you, sweet baby, and I will see you again, at the feet of Jesus, in a world without sin.

Love,

Mommy

Dear Justin,

There were so many things I wish I could tell you, so many things I wish I could do with you. I will never forget the precious times I got to spend with you. Holding you for the first time, watching you fight from the beginning. I can remember how strong your mom was being with you in the hospital. I know how much she loved you. She could not stop talking about you and how precious you were to both of us. I remember when your mom called my work, to tell me that you were going to get to come home. My excitement grew with each minute and each mile I drove. I remember the few nights where we fell asleep on the couch and your mom would wake us up, (w, (well me anyway) to tell me to come to bed.

Days seemed to be filled with new excitement. I remembered the times when you would smile, it brought so much joy and happiness to us. All the little things you did without having knowledge of it, how our little guy brought happiness to not only your mom and dad, but to your brothers as well. They both loved you and cared so much about their little brother. I remember your sweet baby smell, and then I look for your blankets to remind me of how close you are to me. Knowing that I will not get to play with you when you are older, play catch, shoot hoops, or take you to the tractor store which is your brother's favorite activity when we go to town hurts me because I know what's missing. But I know you see it all from where you are, I just wish you would get to do it with them. There are nights when I wake up and I think I hear you cry, it's hard for me, but I know where you are your cry is a happy one, but more of a giggle. Mom and Dad love you with unconditional love. I find myself thinking of you and don't have to wonder what your mom is thinking because I already know.

When I have my rough days I close my eyes and I see your smile, and at that time I feel that you letting me know that everything is going to be okay and that you are safe. I know that you will always be a part of our family, but our family has an angel watching over his family from heaven. You will always be in my heart, my prayers, and always in my thoughts, but I know that you are among the angels in Heaven. Your dad will always remember your first smile, the first time I heard you giggle, and how you made me feel when I held you. You will always be one of Daddy's little boys. I love you little buddy, keep an eye on your brothers, your mom, and me.

Love, DADDY

DEAR JUSTIN,

I love you. I wish we could keep you, but I'm glad you are with Jesus.

Love,

Riley

DEAR JUSTIN,

I love you Justin.

Love,

Jacob

J   is for Jacob and your big brother Riley who love you so much

U   is for the universe; you lit the whole world up with your smile

S   is for the sweet; you are one of the sweetest boys I've ever known

T   is for the times we have shared together which I will never forget

I   is for I love you so much

N   is for never-e-ending love which we will all have for you

We love you so much Justin and we will miss you!
Love your cousin,
Ali

JUSTIN BUSTIN,

Hey buddy; I am not completely sure what to tell you in this letter. I never thought I would have to write a letter under these circumstances, I honestly never thought I would be strong enough to I know the only thing helping me write this letter right now is the strength God is giving me and my love for you. You have touched so many lives in the short time you were here and even now after you have gone. You have helped countless people find Christ in a way they never thought possible. You truly were an amazing little man. You always were one of the most special little boys I had ever met. The day I called your grandma Tjarks back because she had called and said it was urgent was the worst day of my life. The last thing I ever expected to hear was that my precious and perfect little Justin Bustin was no longer living.

In that moment I thought my world was crashing. Nothing seemed right anymore I remember begging God to change it, just let me wake up and it be yesterday, please don't make anyone in this family face this. Well, those thousands of prayers I said in that short time were never completely answered. But this isn't a letter to tell you how much I am hurt that you are no longer with us. This is a letter to tell you how much you mean to everyone you ever had contact with, physically or not, especially me, and all the great memories I had with you.

I remember when your mom thought she was going into labor the first time and I rushed down there as soon as I could the next day. It ended up being a false alarm, but it wasn't long after that you were here with us. The whole time your mom was delivering you, Jack and I took your big brothers to the mall to keep them, and well, us, occupied. We were all so excited. Your brothers kept asking every five minutes if you were here yet and if they could see you or hold you and I was looking at my phone nonstop awaiting a call from your daddy or grandma.

I remember not long after you were born you were sent to Blank Children's Hospital. I rode in the ambulance with you because I just couldn't imagine taking my eyes off of you, being too far away, and letting you make that trip alone. You would stay at Blank for 11 days and I am so honored that I got to spend most of those days there with you. I would not trade those days for the world! I also remember when your mom and dad brought you up to see everyone and the whole time you were here I didn't want to let you go. Other people wanted turns holding you, but in my eyes you were my nephew and I didn't ever want to let go.

Later I had to let go in a way that I will never fully heal from. Even as I am writing this letter to you, I find it hard to see the computer screen through the tears. I miss you so much, my precious little boy. You know I was your godmother - another great honor your parents bestowed on me, and- another great honor that I would not trade for anything. I miss you a little more and more every-day. People sa People say it will get easier but that is only if you push it to the back of your mind, which I find hard to do since you were always one of the first things on my mind anyway. But again I am going back to how hurt I am.

The last time I went up to see you, you were 12 pounds and your chubby little cheeks just made you that much more adorable and cuddly in my eyes. You were being kind of a punk the whole time I was there, though. You would only smile when I wasn't looking, I think because you knew that was one thing I wanted to see more than anything. You always had your own little personality, when you weren't happy everyone knew it and everyone always ran over to help you and see what was wrong. Even the last time I saw you I didn't want to put you down; every time you would cry I would rush overr s and pick you up. Partially because I just saw it as an excuse to hold you and cuddle you, but also because I didn't like to see you cry; but you will never have to do that again.

You mean the world to me Justin, and I cherish every moment I ever got to spend with you and every moment I get to spend with you now when you are with me. I swear I feel you with me sometimes, and those are the only times that this is truly ever a little easier. I cannot wait until God grants me the chance to see you again; I hope you are one of the first faces I see at the end of that bright light.

Well buddy, I am sure this letter is getting a little too long; I could go on for pages about how much you meant to me and still not have it all written in here. Words cannot describe how much that was or how lost I feel without you here. Without being able to call your mom and hear you while I am on the phone or being able to drive up there and see that smiling face (that you didn't like to show me very often) and especially knowing I will never get to hold you in my arms again. It kills me to end this letter, but I know if I keep going I'll drown the keyboard. I love you so much, my angel boy!!!! And I will miss you always!!!

Love you forever,
Aunt Peanut

To My Sweet Nephew, Justin Ryker Swick,

Since you left for Heaven, the lives of those you touched have been better because of you. Our faith has grown stronger, our families have grown closer, and our hearts have grown more thankful. You were, and continue to be, a blessing in more ways than any of us could ever have imagined. Only He could have known what you would do for all of those who knew you, and I know that He knew you were exactly what all of us needed.

For me, your short life and sudden passing brought a new beginning, opening my eyes to the value of life. Prior to your passing, I was consumed by addiction, barely surviving every day. I took unnecessary chances, gambling with not only mine, but the lives of others as well. I hurt those I loved without reason. I took life for granted, every day putting myself, my son, and complete strangers at risk. I was weak, thoughtless, and unworthy. It was through you, Justin, that God touched me. Since your passing I have been sober. I treasure every day like it is my last. My relationships with my family have grown stronger than ever, and my son has the mother he always deserved. Though I miss you tremendously and wish every day that I could hold you again, I feel certain that if it were not for your life, I might not be here today.

Your life, though far shorter than any of us desired, had such an incredible impact on our livelihoods, that your memory will live forever in our hearts and on our lips. Your story will be told for generations, by family, by friends, and by strangers, as the boy who brought us closer to God and to each other.

My love forever,
Aunt Kandi

Dear Baby Justin,

I'm not sure what exactly to say to you, to let you know how much you meant to me, and your cousins, but you were a VERY special boy to us. We only had a few brief days to spend with you, but those days meant the world to us. Just seeing your precious face...the love your parents had for you, the love we all had for you...it was a bond that no one could ever break. The little time we had with you, was not enough, but what it was, was enough to know how very amazing... how very special you were. So special that God needed you more than we did. You were the angel that everyone needed... that everyone loved. Just touching your tiny little fingers, looking into your beautiful bright eyes...we should have known you were an angel that came down here to show us the strength of God's grace. You were loved, Justin. Not just by your mommy, daddy and brothers, but by us all. And now when we look into the sky, we know that even though you are a baby, with you as our angel, and God right next to you...you are watching over us. We love you, Justin....you will always hold a special place in our hearts. We miss you.

Love,
Aunt Feather

DEAR JUSTIN,

You were a very special little guy; you changed so many lives in the little time you were here. There are so many things that I want to tell you, I could go on forever. I remember when I first heard the news of you. I was so excited to hear that you were going to be born. I had never known anyone who was having a baby.

When the date was set I was just finishing welding school, and was offered a job in the city. One of the first things I wonder whether it wa it would be during the time that we were expecting you. I was in the last week of my job and I got the news they were expecting you early. I was upset because I wanted to be there when you were born. When I was on my way home I received news that you and your mother were sent back home and that they wanted to wait a while longer. I was really glad to hear this news because it meant that there was still a chance that I could make it up to see you when you were born.

I had made plans to come up that Friday and during that weekend you were born. I was the first person to know your size and weight; it made your Aunt Peanut really mad at me because she wanted to be the very first to know. We went to the hospital to see you and you were in the nursery getting cleaned up so we couldn't see you wh yet. So While we were waiting for them to bring you back to the room, Aunt Peanut went to get coffee. While she was gone they brought you in and I was able to touch you and talk to you. I was afraid to touch you; I didn't want to get you sick or make Jill any madder at me.

Through the next week I came down to see you in the NICU when I could. I hated that you had to be on the machines; they looked so uncomfortable and like they were hurting you. I would just hope that you would do all the things they wanted you to do so you could get out of there and go home. When you finally got out of the hospital, Jill and I would come down to see you when we could. I always was excited to see you and loved to hold you and see the funny faces that you would make or when you would smile at me and frown at your Aunt Peanut.

I'll always think of the things I could have showed you, like Batman. I wish I could do the things with you like your brothers always want to do an-anything from seeing the cows or spinning them around. I always wonder what you would be like today. What your personality would be, how you would act or what you would even look like. I wish I could watch you grow up and be a part of your life and watch you succeed. I'll never understand why your stay was cut so short. You made an impact on my life the first time I held you and I will always miss you. Look over your family and keep an eye on your brothers.

Love, Jack

Dearest Justin:

I sometimes wonder why God chose to take you so soon and why I didn't take the opportunity to get a picture of me holding you. Although I have no answers, I know that God has a plan for all of us and you were able to fulfill yours in just a few months. You have touched so many lives, which is something many of us take years to accomplish. It made me realize once again, we need to make the best of each day because we don't know how many days each of us has on this earth. If we do nothing else, we need to spread God's love and allow Christ to live in us and through us.

Before you were born I wondered what you would look like and what you would grow up to be. I imagined you to be shorter, with dark hair and loving sports. I wondered if you would enjoy coming to Grandma and Grandpa's like your brothers do. If you would like to spend time with Grandma and snuggle like Jake or if you would rather sit on Grandpa's lap and spend time with him on the tractor or doing chores like Riley. Either way it really wouldn't matter, just being able to watch you grow and learn gave me such excitement.

Even though I can't snuggle with you or watch you ride the tractor with Grandpa, knowing you are in God's arms never having to feel pain or be tempted by worldly things, gives me a sense of peace. So, I guess it is somewhat selfish of me to wish you were still here with us, but I sometimes find myself doing just that.

I know someday God will call me home and we will be together again. I'm not sure what Heaven is like, but God promises eternal life free of pain and suffering and being with those we love. I wonder what you will look like, will you recognize me, or even remember me. I know these are human thoughts, but I can't help but think about them. I miss you so much and long to hold you in my arms and hear you say, "Grandma, I love you!"

Please know I think of you often and you hold a special place in my heart. I love you and will rejoice when I am called to spend eternity in Heaven with you and our Heavenly Father.

Love,
Grandma Tjarks

DEAREST JUSTIN,

MY LITTLEST DEER SLAYER:

We never got the chance to know each other well. The Lord God Almighty must have had a very important mission for you or he would never have taken you away from us at such an early age. As I write this letter I want you to know this is your grandpa's favorite time of year. It's deer season and it's what your grandpa is really a fanatic about. I had dreams that one day you'd get as much enjoyment out of hunting as I do. Something I feel a grandpa should share wand pass down to his grandsons. Though we never got the chance to share a hunting experience together, I want you to know I love you very much.

The hardest thing I've ever had to do was lower your little casket into the ground with your other grandpa. The hurt and loneliness I felt at that precise moment was almost unbearable. I don't believe grandpas were made to outlive their grandchildren.

I want you to know that I love you with all my heart and it's a love that will live in me as long as I live. I will never forget you.

May you always shoot straight and keep the wind in your face.

Luv,
Grandpa Tjarks

Dearest Justin,

There is not a day that goes by that you are not in my thoughts. Your life has touched so many people and in so many ways. God has a plan for all of us and you are one that will be at the golden gates to greet us when we see you again. You are a testament to our daily strength and will to keep going and live for GOD. You have taught us to make everyday count and focus on the important things, like trusting God and spending time with family. You have two super and brave big brothers who love you, along with many cousins who only knew you for a short time but talk about you all the time. You have a special place in my heart and I love you very much. Until we see you again...

Love you always,
Tina

P.S. Your Aunt Tina, Uncle Todd, Cousin Ali, Cousin Austin, & Cousin Ava are sending you BIG hugs & kisses... oxoxoxo's

DEAR JUSTIN,

There isn't a day that goes by that I don't think about you. I have the pictures of Riley, Jacob and you on my fridge. I get to see your handsome little face each day. I remember the first time I got to hold you. I was amazed by the amount of thick dark hair you had. You were a little fighter from day one. Even though you were here for a short time, you managed to touch so many lives. I am blessed for the time I got to spend with you. From your brilliant little smile to your sparkling eyes, your presence was picture-perfect.

I know God has a wonderful plan for you. I have a feeling that you are helping God and Jesus prepare everything in heaven for us. Your assistance was needed in His great plan, until He is ready to call us all home, so we can all be together again. I know when I look up in the sky at night and I see the brightest star shining, that is you watching over all of us. Your Daddy, Mommy and big brothers Riley and Jacob miss you so much, along with all your grandmas, grandpas, aunts, uncles and many cousins. We all look forward to being reunited with you again.

Keep shining your bright light over all of us. We miss you more than words can say and love you always. Do me a favor and keep a close watch over your Daddy, Mommy and big brothers. I know you will. Until we see each other again, my little nephew, I love you much!

Love always
Your Aunt,

Crystal

DEAR BABY JUSTIN,

You were so precious and sweet to Grandpa and Grandma. So loving and cuddly on my shoulder. I could hardly wait to hold you. Your close tenderness has always touched my heart, soul and mind. You were an awesome little baby boy whom God called home to be with the angels and watch over all of your family. Your big brothers were so proud of you. Riley, Jacob and you Justin would have made an awesome football team, along with your Dad. Your brothers loved to hold you. Awesome! Now your Dear Lord has you in His Almighty Hands. I have a star that shines bright in my bedroom window nightly, reminding me of your little life you shared with us daily.

Jesus loved the little Justin,
My little Justin sent into the world for me.
For 89 days, to enlighten this world.
You will always be my precious
little angel in my heart for sharing
this time on earth with me.
Praise the Lord!
Thank You Justin

Love & Kisses
XOXOXOXO
Grandpa and Grandma Swick

P.S. Justin, we were so blessed that your Mommy and Daddy were able to share you with us.

Justin

God had a special plan,
For our little man,
An angel called Justin was sent to Earth
And God carried him home to heaven again.
He brightened oued our hearts with a sweet little smile
and was only here for a short while.
Justin touched our hearts, minds and soul,
to truly make us whole.
You are our special angel in heaven,
I can't wait to see you again,
XOXOXO

Love,
Grandma Carla

Prologue

Life seemed as if it had finally settled down a bit for us. Ryan and I had recently graduated college with our teaching degrees. It had taken me almost six years and I was so glad to be done. Having two kids, working part time and going to school was quite stressful on all of us. We had moved to Alden, Iowa, in hopes of finding teaching jobs in the area, but in the meantime, my husband, Ryan, had found a job locally at Iowa Limestone Co. We figured this would get us by for the time being until we were able to find careers in the teaching field.

We were working hard on getting the house all put together and decorated to our liking. Since I had not had any luck on finding a job, I was able to stay home with our two boys and get quite a bit done in just a few months. This routine seemed so laid-back compared to what we were used to in college. It is a shock to the system when you go from working, being a full time student, a mom, and a wife, to being a stay-at-home mom with no outside career

1

or responsibilities. Although I have to say, I enjoyed those few months that I was able to get things done. While I am still a stay-at-home mom, I almost feel busier now than I ever have, even in college!

With our life settling down, Ryan and I had talked about our future. Where we planned on living, what schools we would send the kids to, how many kids we wanted, and when we would try to have another one. We decided that we really liked where God had taken us and now that we weren't so busy, maybe that was the best time to think about having another baby.

It's hard to get teaching jobs throughout the year so we decided we would wait until school started in the area; that way if I did get a teaching job we could reconsider our decision to have another child.

It's funny looking back on it now, how much we felt like we were in control of our lives. Here we were trying to plan our future, our children's futures, and our future children. It seems so crazy to me now, to think that I was foolish enough to believe I had control of any of these situations!

We already had two boys, Riley and Jacob, both of whom were a "surprise" to us. We thought, "Well, why not try to plan for one this time?

Justin's Jesus

In Loving Memory of Justin Ryker Swick
May 14, 2011-August 11, 2011

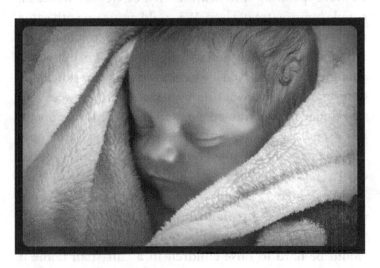

We have always been a mediocre family, living in a mediocre town, working mediocre jobs, and this was okay with us. We have never had big dreams of being rich, powerful, or anything of the sort. We liked our sleepy little life in our sleepy little town. My husband and I met in college, got our teaching degrees, and moved away. We had two children and wanted to raise them in a Christian home. We had both been raised in Christian households and continued to attend church, although I hate to admit that, we did not attend regularly. There were always things that seemed to come up on Sunday mornings, whether it was we had plans, we were spending time with family, or we just wanted a couple hours extra of sleep. We could come up with some mighty big excuses as to why we didn't go to church on any particular Sunday and usually justified it in our heads enough that we believed it was okay to make up ridiculous excuses. My husband at times worked six days a week and on Sunday he just wanted a day to relax. This was one of our excuses we used regularly, even though church only takes a couple hours out of our day, leaving the rest of the day to "relax."

We did have a church that we liked to go to, when we did go: the First Christian Church in Iowa Falls, Iowa. It was only five miles from our home. We decided that it would be hard to raise children in a Christian home if we weren't exposing them to Jesus firsthand by attending church regularly and getting a solid foundation in not only their faith but ours as well. After finding this church, every time we would go, I would call my mom and tell her about the amazing service Pastor T.J. Norman had given that Sunday.

One Saturday I sat in the kitchen, being a brat, thinking, "Lord, why am I praying? It seems like every prayer I have prayed has gone unheard, I feel like I am wasting my time." We went to church the next day to hear a sermon on the Purpose of Prayer. I sat in the pew thinking, "I understand Lord, sorry for being a brat."

There was another time that I was getting frustrated with finances and the fact that we could not find teaching jobs. My husband had interviewed for a business teaching position at the local school and had just found out that he was not chosen for the job. When was it our turn to catch a break? That Sunday the sermon was on finances, living within our means, and the fact that God's plan for us may not be the plan we have for ourselves. Again, "I got it Lord, I will stop doubting you."

When we had our third little boy, we seemed to make up even more excuses. "You know how hard it is to get three kids under the age of four ready for church?" "We're never going to make it in time; we might as well not go!" Our youngest son, Justin, was two and a half months the first time we ever took him to church. We had lived in Alden, Iowa, for over a year and could count, probably on one hand, how many times we had gone to church in that year. I know this does not sound very godly, and definitely not what you would expect to hear from a Christian, but it's the truth and I want you to know I am just like a lot of those who will be reading our story. We were called by God to let you know that even though we were not faithful in giving Him our time, He has always been faithful to us and has shown it in miraculous ways.

We are living in a house that we are purchasing from my grandparents, who lived here for 44 years. When my great grandma died, my grandma took it really hard and was having trouble sleeping. One night when she couldn't sleep she went into the back bedroom to lie down, as to not wake up my grandpa. As she was crying she heard a voice and saw someone standing at the end of the bed asking her, "Why are you weeping when your mother is up in heaven, and I am here with you?" Grandma has always believed in angels, and I believe she was visited by one once after that. (This is just a little insight that will add to the whole story later.)

We have three children; Justin, our youngest, was the only baby we "planned" for, or so we thought. We have now realized that we don't plan anything and that we are living by God's plan. Riley (three-years-old) and Jacob (two years old) are little replicas of their daddy except that they both have light-colored hair. How excited I was when on May 14th (five weeks earlier than "planned") we were blessed with a precious baby boy with a full head of thick dark hair! He was so handsome and was the first out of the three boys to take after my side of the family.

Because Justin arrived so early he had to have a shot of surfactant to help his lungs produce a certain chemical that the body does not produce enough of until the baby is 37 weeks gestation. Other than that, Justin was in GREAT health! He had to be taken to a hospital in Des Moines, Iowa, because the hospital where he was born did not have this medicine on hand. After one dose, we should have been able to bring Justin home, as he was physically fine, and very healthy. We were told it shouldn't extend his hospital stay; instead we ended up having to stay with Justin in the NICU for 11 days, because he was having trouble eating and we couldn't figure out why. On the ninth day, one of the nurses discovered Justin was "tongue-tied," causing him to not be able to suck from a bottle well enough to get a sufficient amount of food to eat. Once the doctor clipped his tongue, he ate like a champ and came home two days later. Justin then doubled his birth weight in just one and a half months.

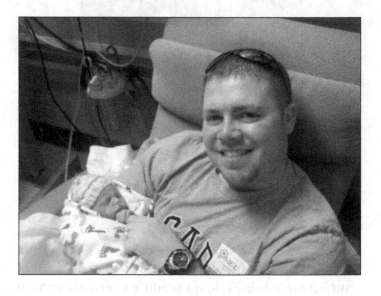

Justin was loved by everyone who had met him. He was such a sweet and snuggly little guy. Two of his biggest fans were his older brothers. Every day they would ask, "Mom, can I feed Justin?" or "Mom, can I hold Justin?" They were constantly telling people how much they loved their baby brother. Riley was especially close to Justin and snuggled him ALL the time! He was so proud to be Justin's big brother and he stayed by his side until the very end.

My greatest fear has always been "losing" a child, and anybody that I am close to knows this. I spoke about it often, and the fear was so nagging that it ate away at my soul and wouldn't let my mind rest. In fact, when my children were infants I frequently had to talk myself out of guarding my heart, because my fear was SO great. It took a sort of power over my life that, at times, made it so I did not want to get too emotionally attached to my children for fear that if something happened to one of them, that I would not be able to go on. I was constantly telling people, "If something happens and I should lose one of my children, God had better take me too," and in a sense He did. He took away the biggest part of me, the

one thing that I had let consume my life, my actions, and
my heart; he took away my fear. What do you have to fear
when your biggest fear has come to pass?

I had been so consumed with fear t tt hat I had lost
sight of God's promises. Somewhere along that road, I had
obviously stopped trusting in God, his plan, His purpose,
His promises. I did this unconsciously, of course, as I had
been working hard on trusting God in all other aspects
of my life. Looking back on it now, my children are one
of my greatest things in life, I know that and if I wasn't
trusting Him with them, was I really fully trusting Him?
The answer is no.

The Bible tells us over and over again, "Do not worry,"
"Do not fear." I was not listening, I was not trusting, and
I spent my life worrying about my kids, my finances, and
my career. Because I was worrying, I was not putting my
trust in God. How freeing it is, to me, to realize this. I now
live my life without worry. I am God's child. He loves me
even more than I love my own children. He is not going
to do anything to harm me. He is my protector, my Savior,
my Jesus, my Father. My children are His children. He did
not take Justin away from me to hurt me, even though,
yes, it hurt. He received him into Heaven with a bigger
plan for him, for me, and for my other children.

I can now live free because of the lessons I have learned
about life through Justin's death. I am more aware of the
need we have as humans to have God in our lives, and to
let Him have complete control. This is a message I want to
instill in my children. All of these lessons had to be taught
to me, just as a parent has to teach a child to ride a bike.
You cannot stand there and hold onto the handles or keep

the training wheels on, and expect them to take them off themselves and start riding a two-wheel bike, on their own. As a parent, you have to let go, take off the training wheels, and watch them fall. Does this hurt as a parent? Oh yes, no one wants to see their child crying, in pain, or discouraged, but what do you do? You stand back, you kiss their owies, pick up their bike, dust off their pants, and encourage them to try again; they will get it. The child gets back on the bike because he trusts what his parents said to him. If the child's parents were to have said to the child, "Oh no, let's put the training wheels back on, you are not ready for this, if you get back on you will fall off again and hurt yourself," that child would trust what his parents said and not learn how to ride the bike, at least not then.

The feeling a child gets the first time he takes off on that bike, by himself, is how I feel now. I am free; I have nothing to worry about, because I am not in control. What is worrying going to do for me? It's going to take away my joy daily, it is going to hinder the time I have here on this side of Heaven because I am not able to fully enjoy my life, if all I do is worry.

That Dreadful Day

One night Justin had wakened at 2 a.m. He had been sleeping through the night, so this was a little out of the ordinary. I picked him up and he sleepily opened his eyes, looked at me, snuggled into my chest, and fell back asleep. Justin had the softest baby hair, and I just loved to run my face across it as I cradled him in my arms. I told him that night, "Baby, I could just snuggle you forever! I never want to let you go." I contemplated letting Justin sleep with me and my husband, but knowing the risks we decided we'd better not, and thought that none of us would get any sleep.

Ryan took Justin upstairs and laid him in his crib. By this time Justin knew how to roll over, and was loud enough that we were able to hear him when he cried. When Ryan had came to bed, he told me that Riley was sleeping in Jacob's bed. Jacob's bed is in the same room as Justin's crib. Riley does NOT sleep in Jacob's bed except when we have company and someone needs to use his bed, and he threw a fit every time that we made him. Earlier that night I had tucked Riley and Jacob into Riley's bed. We said our prayers, read a few stories, and sang a couple songs. "Jesus Loves Me" was one of those songs. When I went downstairs, they were still both in Riley's bed. It seemed really weird to me that Riley would get up and go sleep in Jacob's bed, but I pushed it out of my mind and went to bed anyway.

Sometime really early in the morning Jacob came down and climbed into bed with us. It had been awhile since he had last done this, so I rolled over to let him sleep in our bed. We both dozed off and on for the rest of the morning. Ryan's alarm clock didn't go off that morning, so when he woke up and realized that he had overslept, he jumped up and frantically got ready for work.

Jacob and Riley, (who were now on the couch) both got up around this time also and asked for some cereal. With Ryan in such a hurry, I got the boys' breakfast and went up to check on Justin, who seemed to be sleeping awfully late. Usually Ryan would check on Justin as soon as he got up, again because I was always scared that I would get up there to find something wrong with him and I wouldn't be able to handle that, once again letting fear control my actions.

That morning, my worst nightmare and biggest fear came true. I walked over to Justin's crib, and it looked like there was just a blanket lying there. I felt for him, pulled the blanket off and found my baby with his eyes closed; he was not breathing. Ryan had given me a kiss goodbye as I was walking up to check on Justin, and I started hysterically screaming his name. As I ran down the stairs I willed Justin to wake up, to start breathing, and in the back of my mind I remember hoping to God that Ryan hadn't left yet.

Ryan met me at the bottom of the stairs in a panic at the sounds of my screaming. In a breathless, hysterical, fit I handed Justin, warm and limp, to Ryan screaming that he wasn't breathing and that our baby was dead. I kept screaming over and over, "I knew we shouldn't have put him to bed last night!" Ryan took Justin, said we needed to do CPR and laid Justin on the table. The older boys came in, surprisingly calm and Riley asked, "What's wrong with Justin, Mommy?" Trying to catch my breath while still hysterical, I told him the first thing that came to my mind,

"I think Justin has gone to heaven to be with Jesus, baby." "I want to go too, Mommy." was his reply. "No, Riley, we can't do that right now."

A lot of the next few minutes (although they seemed like hours) are a bit fuzzy. I had called 911, and my mother. The emergency medical technicians (EMTs) were on their way and at some point I had taken over doing CPR on Justin. One thing that happened though, I remember clear as day. When I first found Justin in his crib, his eyes were closed, as they were when I started CPR. I know that muscles twitch, but I swear he opened one little eye, just a bit, and looked straight at me as if he was getting one last look at his mommy and wanted me to know that he was okay.

My neighbor (and friend) came barreling in asking what was going on. "He's not breathing, Jessi! He's gone, my baby's gone!" Jessi told us to get the older boys out of the house, and she took over CPR. I whisked the boys outside, saw another one of our neighbors, and screamed her name, asking her to take the boys. I don't remember if I ever made it back in the house. Ryan ran Riley and Jacob up the block to my aunt's house to have my cousin watch them when the EMT's arrived. We didn't want them to see anything or get in their way. They were out of the house when the EMT's and the paramedics went into the house, and were in my aunt's house, almost a block away, when they put Justin in the ambulance to take him to the hospital.

We rode with Jessi to the hospital crying the whole time and begging the Lord not to take my baby, but knowing in my heart that he was already gone. I believe on the way to the hospital was the first time that I admitted that "all I can see is Jesus holding my baby and Justin looking back at him with a smile." And though this image should be comforting (and it probably was a little, although I wouldn't admit it at the time), all I could think was, "But I want to be the one holding my baby!!"

One of the EMT's who came to our house is also the mayor of Alden. Knowing our family and our faith, he contacted a local church and let the Reverend Bob know the situation. Once we got to the hospital, Reverend Bob and my aunt met us and we prayed. I'm sure we were not there very long before the doctor came in, although again it seemed like hours. The doctor came in telling me that I had "one sick baby," and to be honest it gave my heart a second of hope: "*Sick? I can handle sick!*"

Then he went on to say that Justin's heart was not beating and his eyes were not reacting to light. I didn't want to hear any more, and I told him so. I knew what he was going to say, I understood, and it didn't need to be said out loud to make it real. Down the hall, another doctor must have been letting Ryan know. He was out contacting family and sending out prayer requests. I heard him scream, fell to my knees and covered my ears. What was I going to do now? Now *I* am lost! But I did keep picturing my baby in the loving arms of Jesus. Still a little bitter about it, though. The nurse came in and asked if there was a church in town that we attend, and if we wanted that pastor present. We did! When they called him, I believe he was already at the hospital visiting other patients. This was the pastor of the one and only church we had ever taken Justin to, just that Sunday before. I am so glad we didn't make up an excuse not to go that Sunday.

Our pastor came, sat with us, talked with us, and prayed with us. We would find later that God had led us to the best church for us! The pastor and our church family were the most gracious and supportive people I have ever met. I am so thankful for them and the community. In fact we were trying to think of a way to give back to people such as these that have been so remarkable to us, when our story started to unfold.

Justin's life was short, but we were blessed to be able to do so many things with him while he was here. My husband's slow season at work falls in the summertime when they don't have to produce a lot of feed for livestock. We had just bought a camper and we were doing a lot of family activities together. We would go camping, go to the pool, and just spend time together-a lot of which we weren't able to do during most of the year because of how much Ryan worked.

Justin's Little Life

J ustin met so many people in his little life. My cousin was able to come down during one of her three-day weekends and spend some time with him, and for the first time in two years we went up to Ryan's hometown. We spent the weekend with his parents, his sisters, and their families. I am so glad we did. Justin was the first of my children to get to meet my Uncle Rick from Florida, who came up shortly after he was born. He had not been back in a few years. My little sister and her boyfriend came up and spent a week with us. This summer, I let the older boys stay away from me for an entire week for the first time. At the time, I was dreading them being gone, although I knew they were having fun with my in-laws and their cousins. Looking back on it now, I am so thankful for that week which I got to spend alone with Justin.

That week we went shopping, out to dinner, and took drives just Ryan, Justin, and me. The night before the boys were scheduled to come back, my husband hollered at me to come outside. He pointed out a beautiful rainbow, and the three of us just sat outside looking at it. We discussed how we had never seen a rainbow appear when it hadn't even rained and thought back to the last time we had seen one. We had lived here for a year, and this was the first rainbow we had seen in Alden. It was gorgeous.

The next week we were just getting back into a routine and again spending as much time together as we could because Riley would be starting preschool soon and Ryan's work would be picking up shortly. We had been getting a little frustrated though that my husband and I both had teaching degrees and were not able to find jobs in that field. I am a stay-at-home mom, and to get just any job seemed ridiculous when you have three kids who would have to be in daycare most of the week.

On Tuesday, things seemed to start looking up for us. I love playing around with pictures, and when I got a chance to interview with a local photographer for an assistant photo editor, I jumped at the opportunity. She had recently taken pictures of the boys for us and she does an amazing job. At first I thought the offer was too good to be true! Could I really have a job getting paid for doing something that I not only love to do, but that I already spend my free time doing? Not only that, but I could do it from home!? It seemed unreal, but I was offered the job on the spot! I was so excited! I thought things were finally turning around for us!

Wednesday afternoon I had walked out to get the mail while the boys were napping. When I walked in, Riley was awake and asked me if my Uncle Rick was here (he had only met him the one time he stopped by after Justin was born, and Rick had only stayed for about an hour). I told him, "No Riley, my Uncle Rick isn't here, he lives far away." He told me, "Yes he is, I saw him." I went on telling him that he wasn't here, thinking that he was just being silly. He said, "I really like your Uncle Rick, Mommy." At this I laughed, "Yeah, Riley, I like my Uncle Rick, too." I didn't think much of this conversation until later, and you will understand as I tell my story why this conversation was important. It was also on Wednesday, that I decided to get my camera out and finally get a picture of Justin smiling. Justin had started smiling a couple weeks before, and while I had taken pictures of him during those weeks,

I had never gotten the chance to get a picture of him smiling. This picture is the last picture I was ever able to take of Justin.

Then on Thursday morning Justin went to be with Jesus. When we came back from the hospital we waited awhile to pick up the boys because we just weren't sure we were ready to tell them what had happened. To be honest I wasn't sure how to explain death to a two and a three year old who have never been exposed to anything of the sort except for maybe on some cartoons that they have seen. When we finally decided it was time to bring them home, they walked in the door and we told them that we needed to talk to them about what had happened that day. We started by telling them that we were no longer able to keep Justin with us and that he was in Heaven with Jesus.

Riley started telling us a story about an "alien" in his closet and went on to talk about the ambulance that he had seen at the house (he had seen the ambulance, he was just not in the house). Riley had talked about a guy being in his closet when we first moved in (a year ago) but I had not heard of it since. When I asked Riley who the guy was, he told me that the guy [with gloves] shut Justin's eyes. When we asked Riley later what color the gloves were, he said black and red. (What we decided about the "gloves" was that his hand was shadowed and he had red on them from where the nails were placed during crucifixion.) I wanted to talk to Riley a little more about it, as he was not scared of this "guy," seemed completely comfortable with it, and talked about it willingly. He told me about how he [Riley] turned into a little ghost and sang *Twinkle, Twinkle Little Star* to Justin before he closed his eyes.

We had decided to go to my parents' house that week, because we were not ready to get back to "normal" life without Justin. My oldest sister had given me a necklace that had Justin's picture in it. Riley was looking at the picture as we were sitting outside before leaving, and he said, "Mommy, I miss Justin." I said, "Yeah, I miss Justin too." Riley asked, "Are you sad that Justin is gone?" and I told him that yes, I was very sad. He said very tenderly, "Mommy, I'm not sad." "You're not sad that Justin's gone?" He said, "No, I'm happy." As he was saying this he was not saying it to be mean, so I said, "Are you happy that Justin is in Heaven with Jesus?" He said, "Yes, mommy, and you should be too."

Justin's Angels

had told my family this story and we were wondering if Riley knew what angels were. We do not have a single picture, statue, or anything that would give him any indication as to what they are, what they look like, or what they do. After Justin was gone, my mom had been given a flower arrangement made by a friend with an angel figurine holding a baby; her wings were covered by the flowers. One night I asked Riley, "Riley, come here, can you tell me what this is?" and moved the flowers so you could see the entire angel. He said "Ah! That's an ANGEL! She took Justin away!" I said, "Was this who was in your closet?" He said, "Yes mommy, she flew up and took Justin to Jesus!" There is no way Riley would know that angels "fly up" or that they take babies to Jesus. Later that day, I caught Jacob staring at that same angel. He just stood there for about 45 seconds looking at her. All of a sudden he got this wide grin across his face, as if she were smiling back at him. It was so sweet.

I had written this encounter down as a story entitled "Justin's Angels" and posted it on my Facebook page for others to read. The response to it was amazing! I couldn't believe how many people Justin's story would touch, and to think that this was only the beginning of his story was hard to fathom. I had so many responses to "Justin's Angels" from both people I knew and people I didn't.

A lot of them suggested that I read a book called *Heaven Is For Real*, claiming that what Riley was saying was a lot like what this little boy describes in this book. I had heard of this book, and had actually heard him and his dad talk about the book on the Today Show one morning. I remember thinking, this boy's dad is a pastor, I'm sure he knew a lot about Jesus, Heaven, and angels from listening to his dad's sermons, and I wondered how much of it the little boy actually had "encountered" himself (I would eat crow for those thoughts later).

The next day a lady gave me the book to read. If any of you have ever read the book, you know that in the middle of it there are pictures: some of the little boy, some of his family, and the very last one is a picture of Jesus. I had looked at these pictures before I started reading the book. When I got to the picture of Jesus, I looked at it and wondered why they had chosen *that* picture to depict Jesus It wasn't like any other picture I had seen of him, and I actually had to read the caption underneath to be sure that that *was* who they were trying to portray in the image.

I was sitting at my parents' house with my mom and my sister, and showed the picture to them and asked them the same question: "Why do you think they chose this picture to put in here? Do you think it looks like Jesus? Maybe it tells you in the book why they put in that particular picture." (By the way it does, although I didn't know that until four hours later when I got to that part in the book.) My mom said, "I'm not sure, but why don't you ask Riley who the man in the picture is, see if he recognizes him."

Before I did this, I asked him if Jesus had dark hair like me. He looked at me and at my hair, and said yes, but then went on to look at Ryan, my mom, and my sister, as if trying to see who had hair more like Jesus. He then looked back at me and shook his head, still not very convincingly. "Riley, do you know who this man is?" He got that same excitement in his voice as he did when he saw the angel statue:"Yeah!! That's Jesus!" My mom went on to ask him, "Riley, have you ever seen Jesus?" His response was, "Yes, He put the blanket over Justin's eyes after he died." He had told us once before something about someone putting the blanket over Justin's eyes, but I had thought he just heard us talking about it. (I want to let you know right now that Justin did not die of suffocation, but died of SIDS (Sudden Infant Death Syndrome). When I had found Justin with the blanket over his head I was worried that it was suffocation, even though I knew he could roll over. The doctor ruled this out immediately.)

The book, *Heaven Is For Real*, explains that they had chosen that picture to put in the book because the little boy in the book always saw something wrong with the pictures we generally see of Jesus. Sometimes it would be something with his clothes; other times his hair or his eyes, etc. It goes on to tell you that he had not seen a picture that he felt really looked like Jesus until he saw this picture (the one in the book). The picture was actually painted by a child prodigy when she was just eight years old, who also claimed to have encounters with Jesus.

At that time Jesus, full of joy through the Holy Spirit, said, "I praise you, Father, Lord of heaven and earth, because you have hidden these things from the wise and learned, and revealed them to little children. Yes, Father, for this is what you were pleased to do.
Luke 10:21

I was having a hard time thinking about open-ended questions I could ask Riley that wouldn't sway his response in any way. This book ended up being a road map for me;

I am so glad I read it when I did. I let him go back to playing; I didn't want to ask him too many questions at once, but after awhile I asked him, "Riley, did the angel have a name?" He looked at me and said, "No, Mom, but you know Rick?" "My Uncle Rick?" I asked; "Yeah, I know him." He said, "Like that, Mommy, that's what he looked like". This is where the story from earlier comes into play. I had taken a picture of my uncle holding Justin, and when I got home a few days later I put that picture next to the picture in the book of Jesus. I could see where he got the similarities, as my uncle's hair is brown, wavy and shoulder-length; he has a long slender nose, and bright, light blue eyes.

There were things that happened to others as well, after Justin died. The day after I posted "Justin's Angels," I got a message from our neighbor who works as a certified nurse's assistant. This was the message, copy and pasted straight from the e-mail:

So, I want to tell you about something that happened to me today at work... we have a resident there who is blind, and has been since he was 30 yrs old. Over the past year or so, he claims to see "lights" and people/kids. Sometimes you will walk in his room, and he will just be carrying on a conversation with someone...other times, he's yelling at kids to get out of his room, or for the kids to stop "shining lights in his eyes." They had him see his dr. & and psychologist, and they diagnosed him with... something I can't name at this time, (I don't remember), just that he is having "flashbacks" from before he went blind...ANYWHOOOO. Today, I was walking him out to dinner, and he stopped and said "who was that that we just walked by?" We had just passed the nurse-and she was the only other person around, so that is what I told him; he replied "No, no it wasn't my nurse. Didn't you see that tall man with dark hair?" by now I am thinking he is seeing his visions from his past so I replied to him "No I didn't, but I've been pretty busy. I might have just missed him".... well he seemed a little "sadly upset" when I sat him down, so I said "who is it that you saw?" and he said "you really didn't see him? He was a tall, skinny man, with dark hair, and he was holding a baby" Ok...so now I'm full of goose-bumps, and have tears in

*my eyes...so I ask him... "I'm gonna go see if I
can find them...how old would u say that baby
was?" his response: "I wouldn't give him any
older than 2 or 3 months!" ok- I am now SURE
that he is not seeing PAST VISIONS... I think
this man is seeing angels!????????*

I started praying A LOT after all this happened. I
prayed, "Lord, please keep showing me signs that Justin
is in your loving arms." And for the first time I truly felt
the Lord speaking to me, telling me that Justin was in fact
with him, he was safe, loved, and taken care of. He also
told me that signs would not stop if I would just continue
to listen. It was then I felt like He was giving me a hug. I
had told my sister this, explaining that though I pray often
I have never had the feeling that without a doubt Jesus was
talking to me. There were times when I would pray that I
thought I knew what He was saying to me, but I was never
quite sure if it was just me thinking that's what He would
want or if it were Him actually saying it. The next day, my
sister went to work, and she prayed, "Lord everyone else
seems to be getting signs from you knowing that Justin is
okay, please let me know too." Jill was always very close to
Justin. She stayed with me during the long dreadful stay at
the NICU and she and her boyfriend made sure to come
up every month, generally staying a week. We made them
honorary god-parents. When she got home she told me
her story, about having a hard day dealing with it, about
wondering why everyone else was getting a sign, and how
much she longed for one and prayed to Jesus about it. She
then went on to tell me that as she was getting out of her
car, lying right next to her door was a Soothie binky, the

same one Justin used. She knew right then that Jesus was giving her a sign that he has Justin and he is okay.

Throughout the next few days, I would continue to pray faithfully that the Lord would let me keep this newfound peace in my heart, even though I knew there would be times when it would be hard and my heart would break all over again. One night I was having a very weak moment and let him know, "Lord, I know you are holding my baby, I know that he is safe, and that Your purpose for him is great, but I'm struggling right now. I want to be holding my baby!" All at once it felt as though he placed Justin in my arms; I closed my eyes, and started moving my face back and forth, like I would do when I was really holding him, feeling his soft little hair against my cheek. It was surreal, almost like I could smell him I could feel his weight in my arms, and I could sense the softness of his hair against my cheek. It was then that I felt peace in my heart once again.

> *"The Lord is near to the brokenhearted and saves the crushed in spirit." - Psalm 34:18*

Heaven Is For Real

After I finished reading *Heaven Is For Real*, I asked Riley if he remembered what color Jesus was wearing. He said he didn't, so I asked was it pink, green, orange? He looked at me and gave me his little mischievous grin and said, "Black." I said in teasing voice, "Jesus was wearing black, Riley?!" He giggled and said, "No, silly, he was wearing white and purple…and red!" "Purple? Purple is one of my favorite colors, where was the purple on him?" I asked. He then took his little hand and put it on his chest just below his right shoulder, and said, "Right here." And where was the red? "On His hands and tootsies" (what we call feet).

Everything that had happened that week, what Riley was telling us he had seen, and all that we experienced had given me a supernatural sort of peace in my soul. Though I missed Justin more than I can put in words and more than I ever thought I could miss someone, I was okay knowing that this was all part of Jesus' plan for him, and thinking that I was blessed to have him for even a little while-until we were driving to my sister's house, (nine miles from where my parents lived). That's when what Riley had encountered started to scare me a little.

As we were driving, we were going through a tiny little "town" made up of less than 10 houses on a one-mile stretch of road. All of a sudden Riley started talking about how he was scared of hills. Riley has never been scared of hills, and again I just kind of shrugged it off. Then on the way back Riley said it again, "I'm scared of this hill." "Why are you scared of hills all of a sudden, Riley? You have never been scared of hills before." "A little girl got hit by a car." "You don't know anyone who was hit by a car."

"Yeah, the little girl, I saw the car coming." My mom and I looked at each other.

Riley went on to say, "Mom, that girl is coming home with us." "Um, what girl, Riley?" "Oh, just Grandma," was all he said. When we got back to my parent's house, I went on to ask Riley who he knew that got hit by a car; he told me "Mommy and Daddy." "Not your mommy and daddy, Riley, we weren't hit by a car." "No" was all he said. So I asked him again, "So a mommy a daddy and a little boy were hit by a car?" trying to throw him off a little bit, and he said, "No, a little girl."

The story behind this is that there is a family who lives in that little "town" and about seven years ago, the mom, the dad and the youngest daughter had come up over a hill and hit another car. They all died, and the oldest daughter who was not in the vehicle with them still lives in Mill Grove with her grandparents. Riley does not know this story. I was still at peace with this. The little boys from the other stories I read had also seen other kids. It was what he would tell us the next day that scared us.

Then one day, as we were driving to the store, Riley said something about ghosts being in his room. We just figured he had been watching too much Scooby Doo, but asked him about it anyway. "You mean there were ghosts on your T.V.?" "No not in my T.V.! Out of my T.V. They were green and they told me that I was going to be naughty and play with fire." He was obviously upset, so I asked him, "Was that the night that Jesus was there?" "Yeah," he said, "Well, Jesus protects us from bad guys, Riley; what did Jesus say?" He then told us, "Jesus took them away and

put them in his basement. Then he took me to Jacob's bed
to keep me safe."

By this time even I was a little scared, and I hurt for
him. I was okay with Riley seeing Jesus (and found peace
in knowing that Justin was in good hands), but I was not
okay with him seeing bad things also. I know it tells you
in the Bible that there are demons and angels (Romans 8),
and I know that Jesus protected him, but as a mother you
don't want your children scared.

For a couple days after we got home, Riley would start
crying when we shut off the lights for him to go to bed. We
try to tell him every day that Jesus loves him and He will
always protect him. I prayed and prayed that night that
the Lord would take the fear out of our hearts, that the
devil is the one who puts it there, the Bible tells us that, so
please take it away. I woke up the next morning again at
peace, knowing that He has it handled, and it is my duty
to tell the story.

*"He will cover you with his feathers. He will shelter you
with his wings. His faithful promises are your armor and
protection"*
Psalms 91:4

On my weak days, I have to remind myself that I (we)
are not put on this earth to self-satisfy, and if that were the
case, I could remain angry that I do not have Justin with
me, but instead we are put here to glorify God and that
is exactly what Justin's life and death have shown us, and
that is what we will continue to do.

We went to church that day and read "Justin's Angels"
during the service. We then sang a song about meeting

at the feet of Jesus. I am not a writer, or have never been before, but I came home, sat down at the computer and decided to write a poem for Justin; 20 minutes later this is what I had. I knew that I did not write this poem (again, I generally do not write), but that God had given me the words to put down once I opened my ears and my heart so I could hear him.

The first thing I asked of God the day Justin died was, "Please let Your reason for taking him be something big! I can handle this better if I know that Your purpose for putting us through this was something extraordinary". He did that. With all that He has shown us, in all the ways He has been there, how He has carried us through this, and with as many lives as Justin has touched, He has shown us this.

The second question was, "Why would you even give Justin to me if You just wanted him back so soon? I know that we do not always understand the things You do, and maybe I will never know, but I still have to ask." He answered that question by giving me this poem.

Why God Gave Me You

I sat here questioning why You do things You do?
Why give me a baby and take him away all too soon?
I wondered why God would give me you,
And cried over all the things I would
never get to see you do.
I would never see you ride a bike,
kiss your owie, or fly a kite.
I would never get to hold you again, smell
your hair, or touch your skin.

Of all things He had to do,
Why would He even give me you?
All at once I heard Him say,
"Be at peace, my child.
In My loving arms is where he'll stay.
He was yours for awhile,
But he has always been Mine.
And you are blessed that you had
him even for a short time.
His purpose on earth was great, but in heaven it is bigger
And please, my child, don't be bitter.
Think of all your son has done,
And be proud that I called you to be the one.
The one I chose to hold him close,
For I knew you were the one who
would love him the most.
Your child is safe and waiting for you,
Now it's time for you to do things I ask of you.
If your story you will share, your burden I will bear.
I am with you day and night, feel your
pain, and keep you in my sight."
Now I understand why God gave me you,
And I am so proud of all the things you continue to do.
You have brought people to Jesus
And your testimony never ceases to amaze us.
My heart does not break for you,
For I know where you are,
But it breaks for us who are left,
Because Heaven is so far.
I love you, sweet baby, and I will see you again,
At the feet of Jesus in a world without sin.

"DO NOT WORRY ABOUT WHAT TO SAY OR HOW TO SAY IT. AT THAT TIME YOU WILL BE GIVEN WHAT TO SAY, FOR IT WILL NOT BE YOU SPEAKING, BUT THE SPIRIT OF YOUR FATHER SPEAKING THROUGH YOU."
MATTHEW 10:19-20

I read this verse every time I sit down to write more of Justin's story.

Riley has told us that it was the angel who took Justin and that he (Riley) went up with Jesus. When I asked him what he did when he "went up with Jesus," he tells us that he played with bubbles. Sometimes it is hard to know what a three-year-old imagination makes up and what is real, but he has stuck to this same story the entire time, even the playing with bubbles part. He also told us that Jesus' dad told him he could not stay up there and that he looked for Justin and couldn't find him.

In the books we have read about kids going to Heaven, those kids are not scared and actually want to go back. The difference between their stories and Riley's is that no one actually died. Riley *is* scared; his brother went up and did not come back, and I think that is what scares him the most. He is not afraid of Jesus, and other than the "ghosts," he hasn't seemed scared of anything he saw.

> *37 No, in all these things we are more than conquerors through him who loved us. 38 For I am convinced that neither death nor life, neither **angels** nor **demons**, [k] neither the present nor the future, nor any powers, 39 neither height nor depth, nor anything else in all creation, will be*

> *able to separate us from the love of God that is*
> *in Christ Jesus our Lord.*
>   *Romans 8: 37-39*

The way I look at this trying time is that I have two ways I can handle this storm in my life. I could sink into a horrible depression, letting fear and worry consume me yet again. If I had chosen this route, I would not be allowing myself to be the wife, mother, daughter, sister, or Christian I was called to be. Or I could allow God to take away all the fear, the hurt, the suffering, and the worry and give my life to Him - acknowledging that it has always been His to have.

I foolishly believed for 26 years that I had given my life to God, but this obviously was not the case. *IF* I had truly given my life to Him, I would not have let the fear of losing a child or the worry about what would happen if I ever had to deal with it consume my life for so long. I am no longer living in fear. It tells us in the Bible that sinners live in death but those who are saved live in life. I was living in death. I was scared of dying; I was scared of having to deal with dying, and fully believed that I would not be able to go on if one of my children died. And I wouldn't have been able to, if I did not have Jesus on my side. I have heard a lot lately about how "strong" I am. My response to this is, "*I* am *not* strong, and I still have my very weak moments, but thankfully I have a *God* who is, and He is lending me some of that strength to get through the worst time of my life. *I* am strong because *He* has made me strong and in turn has made my faith stronger."

Jesus loves me, this I know,
For the Bible tells me so,
Little ones to Him belong,
They are WEAK but
HE is strong!

[18] *I consider that our present sufferings are not worth comparing with the glory that will be revealed in us.* [19] *For the creation waits in eager expectation for the children of God to be revealed.* [20] *For the creation was subjected to frustration, not by its own choice, but by the will of the one who subjected it, in hope* [21] *that[h] the creation itself will be liberated from its bondage to decay and brought into the freedom and glory of the children of God.*
Romans 8:18-21

[26] *In the same way, the Spirit helps us in our weakness. We do not know what we ought to pray for, but the Spirit himself intercedes for us through wordless groans.* [27] *And he who searches our hearts knows the mind of the Spirit, because the Spirit intercedes for God's people in accordance with the will of God.* [28] *And we know that in all things God works for the good of those who love him, who have been called according to his purpose.* [29] *for those God foreknew he also predestined to be conformed to the image of his Son, that he might be the firstborn among many brothers and sisters.* [30] *And those he predestined, he also called; those*

*he called, he also justified; those he justified, he
also glorified".*

Romans 8:26-30

I am not scared of death because I know where I am
going and I know that I will meet my Maker and see my
son once again. But while I am here on earth, it is my duty
to glorify God, to tell everyone our story, and show Jesus
to them as He has shown himself to us, through Riley.
Riley shared his story; now it's time for his mommy to do
the same.

> *Therefore, brothers and sisters, we have an
> obligation—but it is not to the flesh, to live
> according to it. [13] For if you live according to
> the flesh, you will die; but if by the Spirit you
> put to death the misdeeds of the body, you will
> live [14] For those who are led by the Spirit of
> God are the children of God. [15] The Spirit you
> received does not make you slaves, so that you
> live in fear again; rather, the Spirit you received
> brought about your adoption to sonship [f] And
> by him we cry, "Abba, Father." [16] The Spirit
> himself testifies with our spirit that we are
> God's children. [17] Now if we are children, then
> we are heirs—heirs of God and co-heirs with
> Christ, if indeed we share in his sufferings in
> order that we may also share in his glory.*

Romans 8:12-7

I hope you all find peace when reading this, especially
those of you who have had to deal with the death of a

child. We all say to people once we hear about the passing of a loved one, "I am so sorry for your loss." I am guilty of this as well. The way I see it, I did not lose a son; Justin is not lost, I know right where he is. He is in the arms of his loving Maker, smiling back at Him, waiting patiently to see his mommy and daddy again and watching over his brothers.

I am the one who is lost, because if I wasn't, I would not be here today to write this story about a mediocre family, from a mediocre town, living a mediocre life that had some huge, incredible, miraculous, life-changing events happen to them in the past couple weeks. It goes to show us that Jesus is not biased; he does not care if you are rich or powerful, if you are a faithful church-goer, or one who makes up every excuse in the book as to why you don't go. He lets us know that HE is faithful, and if you just open your eyes, your ears, and your heart, and most of all listen to the innocent, he will show you the way.

> *Those who live according to the flesh have their minds set on what the flesh desires; but those who live in accordance with the Spirit have their minds set on what the Spirit desires. [6] The mind governed by the flesh is death, but the mind governed by the Spirit is life and peace. [7] The mind governed by the flesh is hostile to God; it does not submit to God's law, nor can it do so. [8] Those who are in the realm of the flesh cannot please God.*
>
> *Romans 8:5-8*

No Such Thing as Coincidence

have come to realize since Justin's passing that there are no such things as coincidences. There were so many gifts that were laid right in our hands the days following his death. We had decided to go with a funeral director in the neighboring town; my mom had already been talking with him getting things arranged for my grandparents, who wanted to get everything done before they died, as to not leave it all for their children to handle. When they asked us which funeral director we wanted to go with, his name was the first that popped into my head.

This funeral home is actually right next door to the church we attend. The first time we met with this man, he told us that it was personally hard for him to deal with infants, because he himself had lost a child: started weeping. He was the most understanding funeral director, very sweet and compassionate. He also did a beautiful job on Justin and told everyone that Ryan and I were his first priorities and he respected all of our wishes. We weren't sure we were going to be able to have an open-casket, because by Iowa law an autopsy is required in any "unattended infant death." We told him how badly we wanted it to be an open casket and he made it happen for us.

We had decided not to take the boys to the funeral, because they really didn't know what all was going on and they are so sensitive to others' hearts breaking. We wanted to give them a better understanding though, and we needed to give them a chance to say goodbye to their little brother as well. Ryan and I were the first to arrive at the funeral home for family visitation; his parents would bring the boys later. We weren't sure we could do it on our own-bringing the boys in to see Justin-so we decided that we would have our parents come in with us when we brought in the boys.

Lenny, the funeral director graciously made sure to keep everyone outside the funeral home until we were ready to start. We went in and saw Justin, and he gave us the chance to hold our little boy one last time. We put his blanket around him and up by his face a little bit, and snuggled him just like we had when we would put him to sleep. I am so glad I got the chance to rub his hair across my cheek one last time. We had contemplated leaving Justin's blanket in the casket with him, and then decided it was the only thing we had left that smelled like our baby. After hearing Riley's story I am so thankful we did; not everyone has a blanket that not only smells like their baby but one that has been touched by the very hands of our Lord Jesus.

When we brought the boys in, things went better than I had anticipated. They really didn't have too many questions. We then let the aunts and uncles come in who wanted to hold him one last time, before we allowed everyone, including the kids, in. Sometime during the visitation as I was crying, Riley came up to me and said, "Mommy, it's okay, I'll get you a new baby, I'll get you a new Justin." Then he walked out to the lobby. He came back and handed me a glass of water. Riley drinks a lot of apple juice, so when he doesn't feel well we tell him he needs to drink more water and that if he does this he will feel better. I guess that was his same logic: Mommy doesn't feel well, let's give her some water to make her feel better. Every time since, when Riley sees me crying, he always brings me a glass of water.

My mom and I ran to Iowa Falls (the neighboring town) the day before Justin's funeral. As we were driving back, the song, "I Can Only Imagine" came on the radio. I had been to a funeral for one of my friends in college, who had died in a car accident. It was the only funeral I had attended for someone I was really close to and being old enough to comprehend what was going on. We were driving my aunt's truck and had never messed with the radio, so it was on whatever station she had left it on. To tell you the truth, I don't remember any songs that were playing before this one came on; I didn't really even realize that the radio was turned on. My mom then asked me if she could show me where Justin was going to be buried. My dad had been given two burial plots for doing some work for his mom years ago. They had talked about selling them because they decided that they would rather be buried closer to their home. He had given the plots back to his mom and told her she could sell them if she would like, and for a year she had talked about it but never did it, (again, not just a coincidence). They gave us the plots to use for us and Justin. Justin is buried at the top of one of the plots so that we wouldn't need to buy another one. He will also be buried next to his great-grandmother.

Ryan's sisters had just sent me an e-mail the night before about a song they had heard that they thought was perfect for Justin's funeral, and it was. The song is called *Held* sang by the same recording artist who recorded our wedding song, *When God Made You*. We no sooner pulled up to where Justin would be buried and this song came on the radio. This song would later help me through a lot of my bad days and my weakest moments. It starts with, "Two months is too little, they let him go, they had no sudden healing. To think that providence would take a child from his mother while she prays is appalling." It goes on to say,,, "This is what it means to be held, how it feels when the sacred is torn from your life and you survive. This is what it feels to be loved and to know that the promise was when everything fell we'd be held." Truly an amazing song! This song fits my life perfectly right now, as I know that the Lord is holding me in His arms getting me through this horrible time in my life. We played this song and *Jesus Loves Me* at Justin's funeral, and both were perfect.

Over 150 people attended Justin's funeral, most of whom I either didn't know or had only met a few times. I could not believe the number of people who drove over three hours to support us on this tragic day. I am so thankful for the people God has placed in our lives. We had decided to get 13 balloons to release at the cemetery to represent the 13 weeks Justin lived on Earth. We weren't sure how many kids were going to be there, but decided that Ryan and I would each release one for each of our older children and the rest we would let the other kids release. As Lenny was taking the balloons out of the bags to hand out, one of the balloons escaped. I looked up at it and said, "Well that must have been Justin's balloon, he wanted to let it go himself." We had the exact number of balloons left to give each child present a balloon to release, including one for Riley and Jacob who were not there with us. God sure does do some amazing things! This is what one of our friends, Rhonda, later wrote us about that balloon. She had stayed at the cemetery after most had gone back to the church, and took pictures for us of where Justin was laid to rest.

"So precious, wish I could've gotten the balloon that went up on its own, a reminder to me lil Justin is leading and preparing the way for that great reunion beside Jesus."

Justin was actually named after this lady's son, Justin Kniefl. Ryan had been good friends with him in school and had worked summers with him and his dad, Bruce. Their Justin was also called to Heaven when he was just 17 years old. His parents have been remarkable, and again I am so thankful for those whom Jesus has so strategically placed in our lives. I did not know Justin Kniefl; however, my husband was touched so much by his life that he wanted to name our child after him. Here is what my husband has to say about our name choice for our Justin, and about Justin Kniefl.

"Little Justin was one of a kind. He was named after one of my good friends from high school, Justin Kneifl, who seemed to live each day to its fullest. His family and I grew close when they moved to town. I ended up working for his Dad (Bruce) for the summer, after I graduated. Justin and his good friend Heath went to be with the Lord, after suffering injuries in a car accident. The impact this kid had on me made a lasting impression. Our little Justin was named after him because of what type of person Justin Kneifl was, a true friend, always happy go-lucky, everywhere he went he made friends. Which is how I have always wanted our kids to be. As I know today that the Justin's were gifts from God, even in their short times here on Earth. Justin Kneifl, the few years I got to know him, left an impression to last a lifetime not just on my life but everyone's life that he touched. I know that our little Justin, in 89 days, was a gift from God. He has touched the lives of so many and continues to do so. I know that they are both in Heaven smiling down upon us. A special thanks to Bruce and Rhonda Kneifl for being like family to me."

Long ago my parents spent a lot of time with a couple, Deb and Larry, who had two kids about the same age as my two older sisters. She and my mom were pregnant at the same time when my mom was pregnant with me. Their little boy was born May 8, 1985, and I was born June

21, 1985. On August 11, 1985, their little boy Jarid died 26 years prior, (to the day) that Justin died. My mom had not seen them in years; they moved to Minnesota years ago. I remember my mom talking about this couple; she talked about them often in fact, and was very fond of them. She would tell me how after their little boy went to Heaven she stopped seeing them as much because she always felt bad that she still had her baby when theirs was called to be with Jesus.

The day after Justin died we got a phone call from Rev. Bob. He told my mom that Deb and Larry (Jarid's parents) were actually going to be in town that weekend; they hadn't been back in years! We got the chance to meet this amazing couple, share our stories, and listen to the advice they so kindly offered us. We were so grateful for this, and it is a moment I will always cherish!

Deb and Larry had arranged a prayer service at the cemetery for their "little man," and another young boy who had gone to Heaven early. It was to be held the day of Justin's funeral at the Alden cemetery where we laid Justin to rest. Rev. Bob would be officiating this service. My parents stayed after at the gravesite to attend. Rev. Bob gave a little sermon and prayer at each grave, including Justin's. I was not able to be there, as we had already returned to the church for the meal that the church so graciously provided for all of us, but when my mom returned she told us all about it. As it turned out, Rev. Bob had said the exact same Bible verse at Justin's grave as Pastor Norman had said at the funeral, although Rev. Bob did not know this. I have seen this particular verse a lot since Justin's funeral. My sister had actually given it to me with a picture of

Jesus holding a baby also and I keep it with me always. I
love this verse.

Psalm 139
O LORD, you have searched me and you know me.
You know when I sit and when I rise; you perceive my
thoughts from afar.
You discern my going out and my lying down; you are
familiar with all my ways.
Before a word is on my tongue you know it completely,
O LORD.
You hem me in--behind and before; you have laid your
hand upon me.
Such knowledge is too wonderful for me, too lofty for
me to attain.
Where can I go from your Spirit? Where can I flee from
your presence?

If I go up to the heavens, you are there; if I make my bed
in the depths, you are there.
If I rise on the wings of the dawn, if I settle on the far
side of the sea,
Even there your hand will guide me; your right hand
will hold me fast.
If I say, "Surely the darkness will hide me and the light
become night around me,"
Even the darkness will not be dark to you; the night will
shine like the day, for darkness is as light to you.
For you created my inmost being; you knit me together
in my mother's womb.
I praise you because I am fearfully and wonderfully
made; your works are wonderful, I know that full well.
My frame was not hidden from you when I was made
in the secret place. When I was woven together in the
depths of the earth,
Your eyes saw my unformed body. All the days ordained
for me were written in your book before one of them
came to be.
How precious to me are your thoughts, O God! How
vast is the sum of them!
Were I to count them, they would outnumber the grains
of sand. When I awake, I am still with you.
If only you would slay the wicked, O God! Away from
me, you bloodthirsty men!
They speak of you with evil intent; your adversaries
misuse your name.
Do I not hate those who hate you, O LORD, and abhor
those who rise up against you?

I have nothing but hatred for them; I count them my
enemies.
Search me, O God, and know my heart; test me and
know my anxious thoughts.
See if there is any offensive way in me, and lead me in
the way everlasting.

    I mentioned earlier that we had recently had our pictures taken. After Jacob was born, we got really bad at going to get our pictures taken, it always seemed like we just didn't have the money for them at the time, or couldn't seem to find the time to get them done. By the time we got Jacob's newborn pictures taken, he was already a couple months old, and the first time that we had a family picture taken of us, Jacob was well over two years old. We really didn't plan on getting our family picture taken right away, but after I had won a photography session for Justin it fell through due to the photographer wanting the baby to be less than seven days old for her portfolio. Since Justin was in the NICU for eleven days she refused to take the pictures.

    We were fortunate enough, however, that our family friend who recently started up a photography business in Nebraska offered to take his pictures for us and took a couple of our family as well. This will be our only family picture taken with Justin. We also had the boys' pictures taken by the photographer I now work for, Steph Stolzman. She had posted a special and we decided more pictures wouldn't hurt. So by this time we had gotten the boys' pictures taken twice in just two months, whereas before we had waited years. One of the pictures she took is also one of my favorites. It is a picture of all three of the boys, however, Riley and Jacob are looking at the camera, while Justin is looking to Heaven.

I also seemed to take a picture of Justin almost every day! I'm not sure if it was just that I had more time on my hands being home all day, or what the deal was, but I will not take a single one of those pictures for granted! This is also, somehow, the only picture I have of me and Justin.

Again I am just so thankful for the people that God has placed in our lives. Stolzman Photography, along with Steph Stolzman has been a Godsend to us and a great friend as well. She has helped us with so many things and continues to be a big part of our lives. She has decided to do a walk in rememberance of Justin near his first birthday. What a blessing! I have thought about different times that would be harder for us with Justin's passing, and his birthday is one I was dreading to deal with. What a great thing though to still be able to celebrate his life and his birth through something so grand special.

After Justin's passing, our neighbor, Jessi (you read about her previously) had bought a little fountain statue when they were in the mountains one year. The fountain has a woman with a little angel baby with a light shining down on them. She had told me that the wing had fallen off one side of the baby and that the fountain hadn't worked for years; she had tried and tried to get it to work. After Justin died she had plugged it in and all of a sudden the water started flowing. She gave us this little statue just yesterday. It is beautiful.

I know that this is not the end of our story but merely the beginning. Tomorrow Justin will be gone for two weeks, and yet it still seems like just yesterday I was snuggling him. It is so hard and at times I really do want to be angry, but I just keep remembering that everything is in God's time, not mine, and that Justin has done so many amazing things. Everything happens for a reason, and I was blessed enough that God showed me His reason for taking Justin early on. I thank Him so much for that. I am not sure if Riley will remember all this, as he is still very young, and to be honest as much as I would love him to remember that he saw our Lord Jesus firsthand, I'm not sure I want him to remember the bad and scary parts that came along with it.

What Death Teaches Us
About Life

D ealing with Justin's death has been a roller coaster ride that I never wanted to get on. Some days I am completely at peace with everything, I am able to listen to the Lord and understand. Other days it is hard, I get sad, but am still able to comprehend the fact that Justin's purpose was so great and that it eases the pain a little bit. Other days, it feels like a punishment. Like I did something wrong and I am being taught a lesson. It is days like this that are the hardest for me. I know that on these days, it is harder for me to open my heart and my ears, take a deep breath and just listen to what the Lord has to tell me next.

I have noticed that when I stop being so determined to hear Him that is when the pain is stronger and lasts longer. I feel that that is my reminder once again, that I am not strong, and if I try to do it alone I will not succeed, but if I remember to listen to the Lord, He will carry my burdens for me. I have bad days, I've noticed, on the days that I am more unwilling to accept the fact that life has changed. A well k-known pastor said it best, when she said, "Our refusal to adapt doesn't change the circumstances, but it does steal your peace and joy." I have learned that I need to keep things in perspective and look at them for what they *really* are. The truth and the fact of the matter is that I was only supposed to have Justin for a little while. God knew how long I would have him and I am so blessed to be given that time with him. Our children are only ours because God has given us them as a gift to us, but they are and will always be His. When I keep my mind and heart focused on this I continue to possess peace but, when I do not accept the change or dwell on the fact that Justin is not here with us physically, it is then that the peace and joy that generally fill my heart diminish I have to remind myself each time my day starts taking a turn for the worse, that I always need to have an "attitude of gratitude."

It is amazing to me what death teaches you about life. I have learned so much about living in the past couple months, there is no way I could possibly put it all down into words. A few of the biggest lessons I have been taught are: to not sweat the small stuff, cherish every moment you have with your loved ones, especially your children, spend as much time with them as you can, make sure to give hugs and kisses every day, to hold tight to the people you are close to and lean on them when you need to, and let them lean on you too. Above all of these lessons though, forgiveness has been the biggest by far! Life is way too short to hold grudges and to let bitterness consume your heart. I was never very good at letting things go in the past, and it has only been since Justin's passing that I have truly felt what it means to forgive and forget.

89 Days

The biggest obstacle we have been dealing with lately is keeping in mind that our perspective and God's perspective are two different things. I know I talked about it earlier, about how in order for me to have peace in my heart I need to get out of my selfish human mindset and stop focusing on what I am missing out on rather than the blessings I was given. A verse keeps coming to me, it seems every day I see it somewhere, is a verse I have already posted:

Psalm 139:16 "Your eyes saw my unformed body; all the days ordained for me were written in your book before one of them came to be."

What I get from this verse is what brings me the most peace. Our days are numbered, just as Justin's were. The Lord knew before Justin was a thought in my head, a baby in my womb, or a child in my heart, that the number of days Justin would be on this earth would be 89. How blessed is Justin that it only took him 89 days to fulfill his purpose on earth, and he gets to spend eternity in Heaven. Justin will never have to feel heartache, sickness, sadness, or pain. He will not have to go through the trials and tribulations that come with being on this side of Heaven. In Justin's life he only knew love. What a great thing.

There have been a number of studies, surveys, and research done on SIDS and through all that there has never been a caused found for why a child would go to Heaven while sleeping peacefully. My thoughts on this are that it wouldn't matter if we had done anything differently that night, if he were on his back or his tummy, in a crib or in a bed, if it was the middle of the day or at night. Justin was only supposed to be on this earth for 89 days; nothing about anything we did would have made God change that number.

My message to parents who have gone through this is: do not blame yourself, the child care provider, or anyone else who may have been present during the time your baby went to be with Jesus. Take it for what it is; our days are numbered; not one of us knows how many days we have to walk on this earth, but please don't take them for granted. Don't waste them by being scared and fearful, worried, hateful or bitter. Be grateful for the days you had your child with you, not sad for the days you won't. Find peace in knowing that it is all in accordance to God's plan and it is far bigger than what we can wrap our human minds around. Keep in mind that our perspective is not right, we have tunnel vision, we see what is here and now, and focus on the pain at hand. Instead of doing this and letting your heart be heavy, give it to God; he knows what the days to come will bring, the joy and the happiness that come out of despair.

We went to church last May, right before Mother's Day. The entire church was sorrowful, as a local teenager had just passed away in a tragic car accident; and we mourned for her mother who would be spending her first Mother's Day in 17 years without her daughter. Pastor T.J.'s message to us that Sunday was, there is a difference between being "happy" and being "joyful." I remember sitting there thinking, "I'm just not sure if my child went to Heaven that I would be 'joyful' in any sense of the word." At the time it was hard for me to wrap my head around the thought. Now that I have a child in Heaven, I understand what Pastor T.J. was saying. I will never be "happy" that my son is not with me physically; however, I can find joy in the fact that he is with his Maker. I find joy in his story, in God's plan for him, and the amazing works that the Lord has done in our lives since. I can say I have peace like a river and joy like a fountain. I miss Justin, I miss holding him, smelling him, touching his hair, but I will see him again and that makes my heart joyful. I could not imagine not having faith; what do parents do then? I have hope for tomorrow for the future of my family, and hope in knowing that I will once again see my son in a beautiful paradise called Heaven. I hope every parent, grandparent, sibling, aunt, uncle, brother, and sister will someday feel this hope, this joy, and this peace.

The other day I was humbled by something that happened. It made me remember what it means to actually be, "held," and "carried" through pain. My little Jacob had fallen down and gotten hurt, and the first name he called was, "Mama." We are in the process of potty-training him and he had gone to the bathroom "big-boy" style not too long before, so he was stark naked. He came running downstairs, and I wrapped him up in my arms, cradled him, caressed his hair, kissed his head, kissed his owie, and told him everything was going to be okay.

This to me is what is means to be "held," as I sat there holding my little two-year-old and consoling him the way only a parent can. I thought to myself, this is how the Lord was holding me when Justin went to be with Him. He knew I was hurt, he felt my pain, he knew it before even I did. I was in his arms, he held me like a baby, caressed my hair, kissed my head, and told me everything was going to be okay. I was being held. Just as I was holding my child that was hurt, He was holding His. Thank you, Lord, for our story-as it calms my soul, strengthens my faith, and puts peace in my heart.

Epilogue

On October 25, the night before my oldest son Riley's 4th birthday, I sat there thinking. This was the first birthday we would be celebrating since Justin passed away. It got me thinking about Justin's birthday, how his first birthday would have been, what we would have done for it, who all would join in the celebration, and what he would look like.

I have a frame on my wall that has a picture of Riley eating birthday cake on his first birthday, and underneath that is a picture of Jacob at his first birthday eating his cake. There is one more slot that is filled with our very first "family" picture. I look at it often, I'm not sure why, but I remember thinking that we would put Justin's first birthday picture there, especially since our first family picture only includes one of our children (I have recently decided to just put a picture of all three boys in there). But I thought how cute it would be to have a picture of each child eating his first birthday cake, all in the same frame.

Now we would not get the chance to have that picture of Justin.

A thought then crossed my mind: *I wish God would send photographs from Heaven, just like we send pictures to family members that live far away, I wish we could receive them from Heaven. I think that would be "fair".* I wondered what Justin looked like now at 5 1/2 months, what he would look like on his first birthday, 5th birthday, middle school, high school... I really wasn't upset about it, I was just wondering and thinking how I thought photographs from Heaven would be an awesome thing!

We found this great idea online, where you fill up a bunch of helium balloons, and on the morning of your child's birthday you put them in his room while he is still sleeping so that he wakes up to a room full of balloons. So the morning of Riley's birthday, I took about 30 filled balloons up to his room while it was still pretty dark out and took some pictures of the room before the boys woke up and then took some more after. I got a new camera and it is a little advanced for me right now, but I took about 50 pictures.

I sat at the computer later to try to go through the pictures, because a lot of them were the same. Out of all the pictures there was just one that stood out quite a bit. It had a huge "glare" in the middle of it and it looked like his room was filled with fog or smoke. I clicked on the thumbnail of the picture to make it bigger and at first it looked like Jacob was standing by the bed; once I thought about it though, I remembered that there was no way he could have been because it was one of the pictures that I took while it was still dark and both boys were sleeping in Riley's bed, and even though the entire bed is in the picture, you cannot see the boys lying on it.

It looked like a little boy sitting in the toy box, when I showed my friend she said, "Mary, don't freak out....but it kind of looks like Justin, he just wanted to celebrate Riley's birthday with him!" (Once I went back and looked through the other pictures, there is a bucket and the back of a board puzzle, and it would be hard to make a person out of either of those.) There are a lot of crazy things about that picture, and I do believe there is something special about it. I don't believe in "ghosts" or "haunted" houses, but I do believe in angels and demons; they are mentioned in the Bible, and with all that went on shortly before and after Justin's passing I have no doubts about that. But whether or not it was the camera freaking out or something else, I will always cherish it as my photograph from Heaven.

Philippians 4:6 Don't worry about anything; instead, pray about everything. Tell God what you need, and thank him for all he has done. 7 Then you will experience God's peace, which exceeds anything we can understand. His peace will guard your hearts and minds as you live in Christ Jesus.

Notes

At that time Jesus, full of joy through the Holy Spirit, said, "I praise you, Father, Lord of heaven and earth, because you have hidden these things from the wise and learned, and revealed them to little children. Yes, Father, for this is what you were pleased to do.
Luke 10:21

"The Lord is near to the brokenhearted and saves the crushed in spirit." - Psalm 34:18

"He will cover you with his feathers. He will shelter you with his wings. His faithful promises are your armor and protection"
Psalms 91:4

"do not worry about what to say or how to say it. At that time you will be given what to say, for it will not be you

speaking, but the Spirit of your Father speaking through you."
Matthew 10:19-20

"No, in all these things we are more than conquerors through him who loved us. For I am convinced that neither death nor life, neither **angels** nor **demons**, neither the present nor the future, nor any powers, neither height nor depth, nor anything else in all creation, will be able to separate us from the love of God that is in Christ Jesus our Lord."
Romans 8: 37-39

"I consider that our present sufferings are not worth comparing with the glory that will be revealed in us. For the creation waits in eager expectation for the children of God to be revealed. For the creation was subjected to frustration, not by its own choice, but by the will of the one who subjected it, in hope that the creation itself will be liberated from its bondage to decay and brought into the freedom and glory of the children of God."
Romans 8:18-21

"In the same way, the Spirit helps us in our weakness. We do not know what we ought to pray for, but the Spirit himself intercedes for us through wordless groans. And he who searches our hearts knows the mind of the Spirit, because the Spirit intercedes for God's people in accordance with the will of God. And we know that in all things God works for the good of those who love him, who have been called according to his purpose. For those

God foreknew he also predestined to be conformed to the image of his Son, that he might be the firstborn among many brothers and sisters. And those he predestined, he also called; those he called, he also justified; those he justified, he also glorified."

Romans 8:26-30

"Therefore, brothers and sisters, we have an obligation—but it is not to the flesh, to live according to it. For if you live according to the flesh, you will die; but if by the Spirit you put to death the misdeeds of the body, you will live For those who are led by the Spirit of God are the children of God. The Spirit you received does not make you slaves, so that you live in fear again; rather, the Spirit you received brought about your adoption to sonship And by him we cry, "Abba, Father." The Spirit himself testifies with our spirit that we are God's children. Now if we are children, then we are heirs—heirs of God and co-heirs with Christ, if indeed we share in his sufferings in order that we may also share in his glory."

Romans 8:12-7

"Those who live according to the flesh have their minds set on what the flesh desires; but those who live in accordance with the Spirit have their minds set on what the Spirit desires. 6 The mind governed by the flesh is death, but the mind governed by the Spirit is life and peace. 7 The mind governed by the flesh is hostile to God; it does not submit to God's law, nor can it do so. 8 Those who are in the realm of the flesh cannot please God."

Romans 8:5-8

"O LORD, you have searched me and you know me.

You know when I sit and when I rise; you perceive my thoughts from afar.

You discern my going out and my lying down; you are familiar with all my ways.

Before a word is on my tongue you know it completely, O LORD.

You hem me in--behind and before; you have laid your hand upon me.

Such knowledge is too wonderful for me, too lofty for me to attain.

Where can I go from your Spirit? Where can I flee from your presence?

If I go up to the heavens, you are there; if I make my bed in the depths, you are there.

If I rise on the wings of the dawn, if I settle on the far side of the sea,

Even there your hand will guide me; your right hand will hold me fast.

If I say, "Surely the darkness will hide me and the light become night around me,"

Even the darkness will not be dark to you; the night will shine like the day, for darkness is as light to you.

For you created my inmost being; you knit me together in my mother's womb.

I praise you because I am fearfully and wonderfully made; your works are wonderful, I know that full well.

My frame was not hidden from you when I was made in the secret place. When I was woven together in the depths of the earth,

Your eyes saw my unformed body. All the days ordained for me were written in your book before one of them came to be.

How precious to me are your thoughts, O God! How vast is the sum of them!

Were I to count them, they would outnumber the grains of sand. When I awake, I am still with you.

If only you would slay the wicked, O God! Away from me, you bloodthirsty men!

They speak of you with evil intent; your adversaries misuse your name.

Do I not hate those who hate you, O LORD, and abhor those who rise up against you?

I have nothing but hatred for them; I count them my enemies.

Search me, O God, and know my heart; test me and know my anxious thoughts.

See if there is any offensive way in me, and lead me in the way everlasting."

Psalm 139

About The Swicks

Ryan Swick works for Iowa Limestone Co. in Alden, Iowa. He enjoys working on cars, watching anything sports-related, and spending time with his wife and kids.

Mary Swick is a stay-at-home mom, and loves more than anything spending time with her family. She is an assistant photo editor for Stolzman Photography in Conrad, Iowa and has recently taken on a few part-time daycare kids. She feels so blessed to be able to contribute to the family income while still being able to stay at home with her children. She would not trade the time she has to spend with them for the world.

Riley is a very energetic four-year-old who just started preschool this past year. He loves school, playing outside, and watching football with his daddy.

Jacob is two-and-a-half years old and he cannot wait to go to school like Riley. He loves playing catch,

tractors, playing with other kids, and snuggling with
his mommy and daddy.